How to Advise The President

21st Century Decision Making

By Dr Graham Rawlinson

Photo by tonynetone, from Flickr

Creative Commons Licence

free to use

Imagine

In her book, Ten Zen Questions, Susan Blackmore takes us through an attempt to 'see ourselves.'

I can see my feet, I can see my legs, I can see my hands and arms, and I can just about see my nose, but apart from my nose, as she says, 'I have a headless body!'

Because we are in our minds, rather than out of them, they are the hardest things to see. So let me take you through an exercise which I hope will help you start this journey of discovery of what may be inside your mind.

This is for no other reason than that you are the start of any and all journeys, and so knowing where you start seems like a sensible thing to do.

At the steps of a monastery there are 10,000 steps to the grand entrance.

Imagine

You could be taking each step thinking: 'I wish they would repair the cracks, I could trip over.' Or, you could be thinking: 'If only they had built bigger steps I could get there in 5000 paces.' Or, you could be thinking: 'I am taking one step at a time, nearer and nearer, to a place of peace and tranquillity.'

Or: 'Nearer and nearer to God', if you are of religious mind. The difference between one experience and another, between the different experiences as you walk up those steps, is massive. Yet in Brain terms, as far as your Mind goes, it will be relatively tiny.

Just a switch, one part on, the other off, a switch between your left hemisphere getting active over the detail on the cracks, over analysing the detail of muscle movement for every step.

Or your right hemisphere taking in some kind of whole picture, the immense history of it all, the enormity of the passion of the millions of pilgrims who have climbed up these very steps.

Suddenly you feel a majestic certainty of the splendour, of the holiness, of the mystery, of enlightenment, of pure joy.

One little switch, on, or off, pure joy, or total sorrow.

This book is an attempt to explore those journeys.

"To bring anything into your life, imagine that it's already there" -

Richard Bach

Bridge Across Forever - A love story.

Contents

21st Century Paradigms

Consciousness and Free Will

Judgement and Decision Making

Reason and Intuition

Ego Minded and Eco Minded Thinking.

Multiplicity

Summary

Context

The 4 aspects of context

Complexity

Collaboration and Competition

Short term/medium term/long term and completion/progress

Risk type

- Catalytic or progressive   Known/unknown ratio

How to Practise your 21ˢᵗ Century Thinking

Process

Tips

How to Advise The President

    Climate Change

    Employment

    Riots

    Health

    Education

    Crime

    War

    Advice to Advisors to The President

Afterwords 1 – Poverty

Afterwords 2 – Ecce Homo

21st Century Paradigms

The most difficult steps to take are those which break the paradigms we have in our heads, and in the heads of our connected community.

There have been some fundamental paradigms through the 20th Century which I think have led to major errors in thinking and decision making.

Errors made by everyday folk and by those who advise the decision makers of the world, as Corporate Presidents, Political Presidents, Chief Executives or simply thought leaders in business, science and art, public and private.

20th Century Paradigm 1. Decisions a best made through conscious decision making, we are free to choose our actions.

Although Freud had 3 levels of mental drives, Id, Ego and Superego, he has been seen as the prime mover in the idea of conscious and unconscious motives, the unconscious yielding all kinds of malevolent and dangerous decisions, including the idea that every accident has a motive.

The paradigm that there is somehow a real us, one without necessary flaws, not driven by subconscious desires, is core to many other 20th Century Paradigms.

Paradigm 2. Reasoning should be at the heart of decision making.

Reasoning was at the heart of 'The Enlightenment'. Reasoning is at the heart of Democracy, and Science, and Education. Reasoning is good, emotion is bad.

Paradigm 3. Our Personality Profiles should match our position in teams and in hierarchies of decision making.

Creative people are good in the early stages but 'Myers Briggs' will help you find the people who will ensure things get done.

Paradigm 4. The exercise of Free Will rests in distancing ourselves from the direct influence of our subconscious desires and the views of others.

Only by seeing things as 'they really are' will reasoning work for the best outcomes, so knowing yourself is about knowing what faults lie in your persona, your profile, but with training you can overcome these and exercise truly free choice.

New Paradigms

1. We are continually conscious at various levels, unless in deep sleep.

2. All mental operations are part of us, who we are.

3. All mental operations contribute to decisions, to thoughts, to judgements, and do so usefully but with potential faults in the system.

4. Reason is useful but has faults, and works best in parallel with intuition, with mutual checks and balances.

5. We are all multiply minded, and there is no singular *'I'* which sits somewhere making decisions.

6. We all have minds which work in collaboration with other minds in other bodies and in our own brain, but also which work in competition with those minds.

7. Free will is not an illusion but nor is it simply a set of executive, independent actions of the mind.

8. Thinking, judgement and decision making *work best* when related to the *contexts* of the situations we are in, for complexity, risk, time scale of change and the collaborative nature of the change.

These different paradigms contribute to a set of ideas about how we think and how we make decisions.

They can be headed:

*How we think about how we think - **Consciousness and free will.**

*How we think about **Judgement and decision making.**

*How we think about **Reason and intuition.**

*How we operate as **Ego minded and as Eco minded people.**

*How we operate as **Multi-Minded people**

*How we think about what kind of thing we are thinking about - **The Context.**

I will cover these in separate Chapters.

Consciousness and Free Will

As a psychologist, Susan Blackmore was interested in her own conscious states and sought to experiment on herself using the meditation practices of Taoism/Buddhism.

She writes eloquently of the difficulties in facing control of her mind and the fundamental significance of these difficulties. Who am '*I*' if I cannot control my own mind?

We have all found ourselves trying to concentrate, trying to focus on something, only to find that that concentration eludes us, we are distracted by things outside and inside, we are not in control of our thoughts.

Possibly, with years of work, we might get a bit better at it.

I would suggest that many of the people interested in seeking new forms of awareness are in partrightly reacting against a false paradigm. That being focused, being attentive is the ultimate state of mind we should seek.

I might even suggest this goes back to Descartes, with his thought space translated as 'I think therefore I am.' It seems as if only when we are aware that we are aware are we *sufficiently* aware to make conscious, free decisions.

So we think that free exercise of will requires control of our awareness yet this is a tremendously difficult thing to achieve.

The answer to this is a new paradigm. It is to drop any sense that one type of awareness should dominate, and to take the view that being ***adaptable*** in how we can be aware of our varying and various types and levels of consciousness makes more sense.

Sometimes, when, for example, checking this document, I should be able to focus, but focus on what?

On the coherent meaning?

On the grammar?

On the spelling?

On the repetition of words and ideas?

When I try to do one I may jump to another, another state of mind, which was also doing coherence processing while I thought I was doing spell checking, perhaps.

So what should I do, what kind of processing should I adopt? The answer comes in the third part of this portrait of thinking about thinking, later in this book.

Programmes for 'Mindfulness' are now fashionable, or Tao practices.

But Tao really suggests the opposite of awareness; the aim is to lose your awareness in order to become more aware without being aware.

The book 'Nudge' is popular because it represents what we may deeply understand to be true, that all we can do is nudge our thinking.

All we can do is shift the kind of processing, perhaps, maybe to being a little more focussed, or a little more open, to being a little more positive or to deciding to be negative in how we feel.

All we can do, perhaps, is nudge our habits in and out a little. That is the extent of our free will.

In saying this I am very aware that many if not most of the psychologists and neuroscientists in this area probably would deny any idea of free will.

But were they free to choose this paradigm?

Try to accept this shift in paradigm.

As you proceed in daily life, be aware only that you shift levels and states of consciousness all the time, and that many are operating usefully.

The implication seems to be a pretty good one, which is to relax and enjoy the ride, trust that thinking is going OK and that only from time to time, when the context tells you to, should you, and even could you, stop and check your thinking processes.

Judgement and Decision Making

If we accept the paradigm about multilevel consciousness and its usefulness, then we should examine again how we see decision making.

Decisions seem to be made as 'extensive' activities in the brain rather than as concentrated/'intensive' activities.

That is, they are not made as a sequence of events so much as an orchestra of neural motions in harmony and disharmony, what happens happens.

What makes a big difference is something I would call judgement, which is how the various associations between different neural patterns are weighted, weighed.

In that weighing process they create judgements which themselves through the chaotic neural activity lead to decisions.

The decisions emerge from a combined value and meaning of the network of connections.

If they are coherent then they possess meaning, and the value of one set will pass value to another set if they are meaningful.

Even when rapid decisions are made it is because many sets of responses are available and they get triggered by some kind of neural element.

Oxtails and Oxitalis - Value and Meaning

While writing my books in Spain, I was also trying to improve my Spanish and to learn more about herbs. It suddenly occurred to me that my struggle was to do with value and meaning.

Sometimes people with Autism 'recover' from the early, very traumatic years. They can then talk about what it had been like and how they are still a little different from other people.

They still may seem a little odd, but often not so much that you would think they had any kind of severe disorder.

Some time ago I listened to a woman with Autism being interviewed.

She seemed to be saying that the signals, the input, had no value(s), and therefore she did not find any meaning in the signals.

Autistic children either want the signals to stop or they want to make other signals which because they created them have some kind of value, some kind of meaning.

It is a bit like when someone else is using a drill or a vacuum cleaner, it is very noisy, but when you do it yourself it is much less noisy.

The point is that it is not that because it has no meaning it has no value, it is because it has no value it has no meaning.

All noises, all sounds, then have the same kind of *irrelevance*.

As she got older she slowly found some value in the sounds and then some meaning. For some Autistic people a life full of meaning emerges from the noise.

Unfortunately for many this does not occur.

And this is my problem with learning Spanish, at first at least.

Looking through my books on herbs, I have the same problem. I can see and read about the shapes and colours and sizes or the leaves, the stems, the flowers, the roots, but I don't know how to *value* the information.

I can learn that one plant is 4 cms across, but then I find so many others are also about 4 cms across. The book on herbs does not guide me to things of value.

It just noisily describes things.

In one of his great books, Richard Feynman (perhaps the greatest physicist of the 20th Century) describes trips into the countryside with his father.

His father did not name the birds they saw, he did not know the names of the birds.

But they examined the movements of the birds, and deduced the differences in those to understand how the birds were all different.

They valued things which in education we normally don't value till much later. I need a herb book which helps me value the differences for when I am cooking.

Going through my Spanish Grammar book I also find I am searching for what to value and what to leave to one side.

For some words the stem is clearly the value attribute, and changes at the end are of little significance.

For other words it is hard to know what the stem is. Hago, hice, hare, are all from the word Hacer, to make. Similarly, He, hube, and haya belong to the word Haber, to have. I can try to learn these but somehow I need to find value in them and then meaningful connections will be made.

I find it hard to remind myself to find these words important.

When at school teachers put great stress on knowing whether the word for 'table' is masculine or feminine, in French and Spanish. This is something native English speakers find hard to value. It is hard for us to believe that the difference is of value.

At all levels of business, people need to understand what has value, whether for the sales assistant and the customer, the stock replenisher in relation to the display, or the marketing and finance directors in relation to sets of numbers to do with market share, margins and profits.

I wonder whether in teaching business studies we are sometimes trying to impose meaning on situations without helping people to understand the value of the features of the market place?

The problem ultimately is inflexibility.

Having understood, or learned, what to value and building that into something with 'meaning', people find it hard to change how they see the value, just as we find it hard to learn a second language after the age of 5 or so.

We have become tuned to the perceptions we feel we should value, and the values then deliver the meaning.

A careful review of the Left and Right hemispheres is needed from time to time. LH or RH? Or both?

The RH is where we find meaning, but that meaning has come from LH input and selection, so sometimes we need to go back to the detail, to ask again what input really now has value; maybe that has changed.

Numbers may change and values may change, they are not fully linked.

When we go back we need to challenge the current sets of values. One way to do this is by making them very abstract, a LH game.

Or, we can play RH games, we can pretend to change the values of attributes, and see how that feels. Are there new details out there which challenge and change our value system completely?

Summary:

Meaning derives from the *values* we attribute to the *features* of things. This meaning can lock us away from revaluing those values.

We can usefully challenge this from time to time (not too often) using exercises with the Left Hemisphere and the Right Hemisphere.

Reason and Intuition

So Judgement, which means attaching **Values** to things, to *thoughts* about *things*, leads to decision making. So where do Reason and Intuition fit in?

The old paradigms were assisted by a parallel paradigm on reasoning.

To use reasoning we must be using some kind of focus, and an awareness of that focus.

If we were not aware of how we are focussing how could we know we are focussing, and not drifting off somewhere, with thoughts driven by deep unconscious desires?

This kind of thinking is normally associated with operations of the left and right hemisphere and a new interpretation of how the hemispheres work is in Iain McGilchrist's book, The Master and his Emissary.

He raises concerns about the dominance of focussed thinking.

As McGilchrist rightly says, most operations are split across both hemispheres and front to back and top to bottom, but nonetheless there is a real functional difference in the sections of the brain we should be aware of and take account of.

For a beautiful report by McGilchrist on his ideas see an animation following him speaking about the hemispheric split - http://www.youtube.com/user/theRSAorg#p/u/1/dFs9WO2B8ul

This old paradigms of thinking about consciousness and awareness and focus and reasoning is being challenged in a number of directions.

Gigerenzer's book Gut Feelings promotes the idea that in many situations to rely on or even use reasoning is faulty.

Jonah Lehrer, in his book How We Decide, calls the pre-frontal cortex, which is also key to focussed decision making, a 'cheap calculator.'

Another challenge to the idea that focus and reasoning are to be sought as the best manner of thinking comes from studies which strongly suggest we do not have free will anyway.

Analysis of 'decision paths' in the brain clearly suggest that decisions are made *before* you are aware of yourself making decisions.

So it seems you cannot stand aside and reflect and then somehow choose.

You can stand aside, you can reflect, but the only choice you have maybe whether to decide this was your choice or just a decision which came to you out of the blue.

Reasoning cannot really be dominant if we don't have the ability to make a free choice at the end of the reasoning!

The development of science is closely linked to the development of this kind of focussed thinking and reasoning.

The process of science for several centuries has usefully been to segment everything, to look at smaller and smaller pieces and to decide how the sequences work together.

But in many fields it seems as if the extent of the value of segmentation is dropping, it is more useful to look at multiple attribute causation, where many things depend on many other things for the outcomes which result.

This matches more our real experience. Whether buying a bar of chocolate or a house, or employing person A rather than B, there is no single trigger, almost never, it is all about multiplicity of actions and contexts.

With that kind of new thinking, with the dominance of reason coming into question, people are beginning to examine where reason works well and where intuition works well, and likewise, where there are faults in the processing.

Where intuition scores is when reality is complex, so without some way of bringing the multiple attributes together and 'scoring them' putting them into some kind of weighing scales, the brain does this magic job of using intuition and comes up with telling you what it 'feels' is the right thing to do.

Some pretty good experiments show that intuition can be much better than you might suppose, and certainly way better than reason, even when some numbers are involved!

A simple example would be whether to eat an apple or a pear. There are complex facts of chemistry, rate of deterioration of product, change of taste over time, potential as a food hazard and so on, facts cannot drive the decision. They are more likely to falsely distort the decision.

Why do acorns fall off trees? – Good and not so good practice in scientific thinking

Let's examine science and focussed thinking for a while with this seemingly simple question about acorns.

We can give the answer 'because evolution makes them available for the next generation of oak trees'.

Or we could give the answer 'because the cold weather triggers the complex chemistry of the trees to release a substance which hardens the connection between the acorn and the tree, so when the wind blows the acorn is released and travels further.

Or we could give the answer, to feed the squirrels. And so on.

Each of these answers is what the Reverend Bayes called varying hypotheses. The mistake we make is to see this Bayesian approach as helping us find the *correct answer* as if there is just one.

The reality, however, is that different answers are really *opportunities* for an emergent new way of thinking, a new kind of learning. It is the multiplicity of answers, true in varying degrees and varying contexts, which yield new options.

When we are faced with the question, 'why do acorns fall off trees' we can choose to attempt to find a singular answer which satisfies the bean counter in our heads.

The bean counter is mostlyin the left hemisphere, LH for brevity.

Or we can choose to attempt to build a holistic view of all the possible answers, which yields a more satisfied RH.

There is the danger that the RH can be satisfied with a whole picture without much detail and then science might not progress too well.

So the question we ask ourselves when faced with a question is how to balance the LH's thinking and RH's thinking, knowing the mistakes both can make and the benefits each can bring.

When we now face some big question like how do we create full employment, or how do we reduce crime, or how do we create a community committed to learning, the first question, the first type of choice, is how to weight the judgement of the LH and the RH.

Another list that may be useful when trying to think about how thoughts may or may not be scientific is this:

1. What is meant by...? - Identifying points beneath points and looking for a better understanding with both hemispheres.

2. How does it explain these bits of *evidence*? And what does *explanation* mean?

3. What are the assumptions behind these points?

4. Does the concept help us 'understand' things?

5. If it is right, why doesn't it feel right? And why does it feel right?

6. Is the explanation simply the fashion of the day?

These points seem to me to be at the heart of all science, and maybe should be in if not at the heart of all thinking, well, thinking about thinking. But they all require a mix of LH and focus and RH and holistic feel. Even point 6 can be explored using focus or big picture feel.

That checking also means truly listening to what other people say, and also what other minds you have in your head say, and so we move on to the next section.

Ego Minded and Eco Minded Thinking

So, Decisions emerge from the Values given to things by Judgement processes, which are affected by various levels of Awareness of those things and our processing using Reasoning and Intuition.

Our control is not of the outcomes but of the extent to which we use those processes, the extent to which we raise our rational and intuitive awareness of those processes.

We have some control of process but not outcome.

This might seem minimally satisfactory to those who feel a need to be in full control of their own decisions and actions, but there is worse to come for those people.

We have Ego Minded Thoughts, and associated Values.

We also have Thoughts and Values deeply embedded in the thoughts and values of others, all those people who interact with us, the real face to face, the technology assisted, and the virtual!

I call this Eco Minded Thinking, we think in cross connected communities.

To begin with we have the idea of memes. A **meme** is "an idea, behaviour or style that spreads from person to person within a culture."

"A meme acts as a unit for carrying *cultural ideas, symbols or practices*, which can be transmitted from one mind to another through writing, speech, gestures, rituals or other imitable phenomena."

"Supporters of the concept regard memes as cultural analogues to genes in that they self-replicate, mutate and respond to selective pressures."

This is from Wiki.

Richard Dawkins coined the word in 1976 in his book, The Selfish Gene. It has gained general acceptance in its light form, that ideas have some kind of evolutionary survival principles behind them.

But the idea of memes becomes much stronger if we add the idea of 'mirror-neurons'.

It seems that when we see someone else doing something our brains map a mirroring of that action as it occurs, which gives us insight and empathy.

We can even practise skills by imagining someone else doing something!

Now think again about our own self-control, or lack of it, our own varying levels of consciousness, of how the values associated with thoughts lead to judgements which result in decisions.

If we combine this with cultural memes, we can see that being Eco Minded is to fully recognise that the immense number of mental events passing through our heads do so with 'lives of their own'.

We are vehicles of internal and external thoughts, and the only thing we can control is the process of engagement with those internal and external thoughts and the values associated with the thoughts.

So in thinking about our thinking the Paradigm change is to see ourselves as both singular and plural in how our thoughts exist in our heads and in the extended heads of others.

The 'collective consciousness', if we can put it that way, can be thought of as the 'wisdom of crowds', and certainly should not be thought of as inferior.

But crowds can also be collectively stupid, so to balance that we do need our singular selves, the selves that can take on a single perspective which helps get things done.

Or the singular self just helps take away the smoke and mirrors that crowd thinking can generate, with its cults, membership clubs and associated symbols of 'truth.

Multiplicity

A key *paradigm extension* to Eco Mindsis into the idea of 'multiplicity'. This is the idea that our brains do not develop just one 'persona', but most often many persona.

This means that it is not simply that we have different moods, or that we play act different people at different times, or that we change as we grow older.

The different persona are meaningful in that they have different memories, different motives and different skills. These ideas were discussed extensively in the In2In Dialogue on….. with myself and Rita Carter, author of the most recent book 'Multiplicity.'

The rationale for having different persona is that it aids survival value.

Rather than having internal mental conflict when faced with different scenarios, the mind simply switches from one persona to another.

So motives change, memories change (you don't want bad thoughts intervening when you have a different agenda) and even skills change (ask any golfer entering a tournament.)

So It 'makes sense' that we are multiple. Interestingly, one of the founders of the idea of being multiple was

William James, who was one of the founders of psychology itself.

Somehow the idea got dropped.

Incidentally, this also challenges much of the business of identifying our 'personalities', what we probably get from 'personality tests' is an identification of the persona that does personality tests.

But nothing is offered on the other persona we adopt from time to time or could adopt if we were prompted to do so. Personality tests are based largely on the paradigm of the singular self. The fundamental you.

So maybe HR departments are missing a huge set of resources, all those other persona who could do different jobs but never get called into action.

Or, at the other end, all those other persona who disrupt and sabotage projects because they never get recognition! Consciously or unconsciously of course.

The idea that we should deploy our different persona to suit different tasks again seems sensible enough, it is a different paradigm, and then we can add one more level, which relates to teamwork, leadership, people management.

If each person available could be any one of several different people, how would you then build a team and lead and manage it? It opens up all kinds of new possibilities.

And we have one more step again, the paradigm extension which says that much of the time the thoughts you have, have an extended existence outside of all of your persona.

In its simplest sense we have 'memes', which like genes have their own survival processes, some kind of extended survival of the fittest.

But more than that, just as evolution is not necessarily as simple as it first seems, so thoughts, ideas, even paradigms, exist within a context of other thoughts, ideas, and paradigms.

It is the overall collaborative and competitive ecology of the system that leads to some surviving and growing while others die.

So the reality is that within our own persona, within the varying persona of the groups with which we interact, and within the more nebulous cross connected multiply minded networked of connected thought engagements, we have thoughts, idea and paradigms each living and breathing inside and outside our heads.

In terms of reasoning and intuition what this means is that the values we place on the procession of thoughts in our heads is constantly changing.

The way in which those thoughts are connected is also constantly changing, as are the values of those connected thoughts because each new connection brings positive and negative attributions.

It is all one very alive kind of process.

Whilst the value of intuition in seeing/getting the 'big picture' can be recognised, the danger is also there, not only can there be a constant flux of values in the big picture but from time to time the big picture can change but will it change for the better?

Will too much change lead to never getting anything done?

So one value in having reason is to stabilise the picture.

Its value is to create what is essentially an artificial structure, with a very poor set of true value attributes, the value attributes which can't tell good stuff from bad stuff, but at least will get you to stick to things and get something done.

And then the bad thing about reason is that it will get you to stick to things even when any proper 'value attribution' would make it clear that the whole thing should be abandoned, in the end, too many soldiers die fighting the same battle again and again.

The Best Way to Slim –(or cut down on anything)
- change the size of your plate!

Most people who want to lose weight probably try some kind of slimming diet. The diet suggests how much you should eat of all kinds of different things, and of course some diets are the opposite of others, carbohydrate high or low, no meat or all meat and so on. In fashion at the moment are diets that ensure enough fruit and veg, fibre and vitamins and minerals.

The trouble is that this is very much a LH approach, lots of detail, lots of precision, a plan, a process. And feeling hungry, of course, is a feeling.

Another approach is to simply change the size of your plate. Use a side plate instead of a dinner plate, and when you have it in front of you it will *feel* like a lot of food.

It won't stop you snacking and you still need to buy fruit and veg and stuff, but for most people just changing the size of the plate will do it.

I am thinking about how this compares to project management. Generally. One big part of project management is planning of budgets, which is a bit like planning a diet and has the same kinds of problems.

Budgeting is seldom a well 'managed' process. It has all the features of bad diets, bingeing, treats, waste, and general excess or shortage.

Suppose you have a budget of 1 million dollars for a 12 month project. It's hard to know how to handle the budget. You have a project spending plan with patterns to cover different features, all very theoretical though.

Things come up which are unexpected, so you use the contingency budget, some things cost more some less.

Budget spend should be analytical but often it feels more like a wing and a prayer?

It should be all LH. Facts, analysis, but it often is about how it feels the spending is going, a gut feel as to whether you are going to be over budget or under.

The feel of having a million dollars to spend is not the same at the beginning as having just 50,000 at the end, of course.

It is not just that the numbers are different, it is that one is looking ahead and the other behind, mostly, which means there are two different people doing the job, and there should be.

The person looking back should have some concern about how the numbers went, are the figures in the right place, that kind of thing.

But the process of looking back should be holistic; it should be getting a feel for how the whole thing went.

There is no definitive answer as to the right and wrong of the spending, maybe a bit here and there, but a lot of the time the value to the project of spending this bit and that bit of money will never be clear, BECAUSE IT IS NOT AN OBJECTIVE THING!

As project manager you may well have changed your persona as the project went on (to the annoyance of those working with you). You started of all miserly, and at the end you were a spendthrift.

Or the other way round. It is often the change of persona that annoys people, and people are not clear how they should act, whether they should put more time into saving money or getting the job done on time and to the spec needed or planned.

Maybe you take on the idea of changing the size of the plate. What if you have a spend limit of 30,000 dollars each week?

Some thing may cost 90,000, so you have to 'save up for them'! So you get more of a feel of the money to be spent, not just a signing off of the purchase.

So you allocate 10,000 within your own internal budget, to make it feel like you are spending, or at least limiting other spending.

You feel the pain of waiting, the LH meets up with the RH!

This may seem like playing games but your brain is playing games anyway, you just don't want to admit it.

OK, so exceptions might be needed, but you would 'feel' the exceptions being made, they would not just be meaningless numbers on a spread-sheet.

The aim of course is to assist your judgement, there is no right and wrong on spending money, well, maybe some things are wrong, but mostly no absolutes.

The idea of changing the size of your plate pushes you into a mind state which recognises the relative size of a spend on a regular basis, a weighing up of priorities.

At first it will feel like more work but this is because you are doing work that would normally come later or doing work that should be done but has not been done in the past.

Creating tools to help the RH, seeing the whole, is surely a good idea.

Any more chips anyone?

How Children Think

Even though we were all children once, we have very little idea, as teachers, parents or just by-standers, about how children think.

We have agreed mind games we play, with rules established, which give children security, reducing unpredictability, but we don't really understand in depth how they think.

They are foreign territory.

In 'To Kill a Mocking Bird' by Harper Lee, we have the deeply true statement that 'you never really know a man until you stand in his shoes and walk around in them.'

The important thing in the statement is not simply the acquiring the temporary perspective of the other person, it is the dynamics of that person's life, walking around in his shoes.

It is not enough to know that once you were a child and can therefore see things briefly as a child does. To know the child we have to be in their shoes and walk around in them.

In the book by Harper Lee, 'Scout' says (and she is just 8 years old) "Jem and I would get grown up but there wasn't much else for us to learn, except possibly algebra."

So the child is able to see the whole thing and now, just needs to acquire 'minor details.'

But to see this we would have to return to being in the shoes of the child, and walk around in them, and as with all our full experiences, we would have to feel how the whole world is out there but part of us.

It has not separated into things known and things unknown, not as feelings of separation.

This only happens, 'when we learn algebra.'

The great advantage in being multiple is that we get the chance to walk around in different shoes. That is why Multiplicity exists, it has a functional purpose.

If we push a paradigm on people, when they are growing up or when they hit adulthood and jobs and careers, that they should somehow be an identifiable single persona then we are reducing their ability to have some opportunity to be on the inside of others, to feel that true empathy that comes from walking around in their shoes.

So whether it is IQ or EQ, whether it is a suggestion of neurotic or compulsive, whether it is Libran or Gemini, they are all narrow and old paradigms and unsuitable for the people of the 21st Century. Get with it, get multiple!

Summary

It is the collection of attributes which creates a collective aggregation of values which constitute judgements at various levels, in a multiple cross connection of minds.

In the end the decision has final value through some use of reason and intuition, but never reason alone.

Your job, as owner of your own thoughts, ideas, judgements and decisions, is to manage the process of thinking, bringing balance into the operations.

How you do this depends on context, which is what we look at next.

Context

To ensure that a better understanding of thinking and decision making can be applied, there is a need to reflect on the kinds of conditions that our thinking and decision making processes have been designed, by evolution, to adapt to.

A simple map is enough for now, though a greater degree of sophistication is possible. We only have a certain amount of time to reflect on our thinking and decision making, so to begin with let's keep it simple.

For more detailed review of thinking, it is recommended that people work with the processes of Synectics, TRIZ, as outlined in How to Invent (Almost) Anything, by David Straker and Graham Rawlinson.

This can be read alongside a broader exploration of thinking and feeling in the novel, Judgement Day, by just me, Graham Rawlinson.

The 4 aspects of Context

1. Complexity
2. Competition and collaboration
3. Short term/medium term/long term and completion/progress
4. Risk type – catalytic or progressive, known/unknown ratio

Complexity

There are many ways of looking at complexity, and in some ways it is possible to say that you can never know how complex a situation is, you may have missed a simplification which reduces everything to simple in one Eureka moment.

Archimedes found a simple way of measuring the weight of gold, and Galileo reduced the complex orbital motions of planets by offering the paradigm that the Earth travels around the sun.

Even in what may seem horrendously complex situations there could be a simple solution.

Reducing street crime might seem a multilevel problem of societal attitudes, systems of detection and punishment, education, religious attitudes and more.

But it is possible that a simple advanced CCTV camera cuts overall street crime in half.

Making a decision on how complex a situation is becomes important when you try to explore which mind tools are best for the job.

Even though there can be no absolutely certain 'right answer', a judgement needs to be made and decisions follow on how to adjust your thinking accordingly.

So stage 1 in your thinking is exploring the nature of complexity of the situation, and as the outcome of that exploration might vary from a judgement of 'massively complex' to 'totally simple' an open ended exploration is where you should start.

You can use any set of tools for this, any creative process for wandering through possibilities.

Maybe de Bono's Lateral Thinking or Synectics or CPS or Storytelling or Storyboarding.

At the end of the process, which is usually best done in groups, with a facilitator, you sit back and let your inner judgement suggest whether it is simple or complex.

Occasionally the task might be so important you want to try both tracks, and for this the best approach would be to have two teams, one seeking the simple solution and the other trying to explore the complex features and see where they lead.

For example, if you decided that reducing obesity levels was probably a complex problem but the savings and benefits from finding a simple solution are worth some level of investment, then you might have two teams.

Either of these may become redundant depending on the outcomes each produce.

We can now explore how we would treat simple and complex problems, starting with simple.

Problems which are believed to have or may have simple solutions

There are two types of simple solutions.

The first is the solution that is obvious as soon as you see it, so the process is one of searching, and conducting the search in such a way that you look for it everywhere and you spot it when you find it.

It might seem like contradictory to suggest that you have to ensure you spot something that has been defined as obvious when you see it, but it depends on what is meant by seeing it.

If I am looking for a screwdriver and see a spoon which has an end which is just like the end of the screwdriver, I may see the spoon but not see it as a solution to the search.

Once I see it as a solution it is only then obvious. So the definition of obvious is 'obvious when you see it as the solution.'

For the 'obvious' when you see it solution you can use open exploration processes, like Synectics, or you can use systematic search processes, such as TRIZ. The choice depends on the risk of not finding something that is there.

That is covered later.

The second type of simple solution is the one which requires substantial revamping of the constructs, features, attributes of the system before the solution is wrung out.

If the revamping is of the major premises of the context for the solution, then a highly challenging open process may be used.

Synectics uses processes which will challenge all basic tenets where necessary.

If the revamping is complex towards the solution end, so it is a problem where you keep getting close to a simple solution but not quite, then the very substantial closure processes of TRIZ may be preferred.

Problems which are believed to have only complex solutions

Where the type of problem being faced is complex, the processing of that complexity is as much about how to value the costs and benefits of the potentially infinite number of different actions that can be taken.

In this situation, the major mind processing will be related to the right hemisphere, it will be holistic thinking that needs to be core to the process.

The reason for this is to avoid the big picture being diverted by potentially rather irrelevant facts. The 'cheap calculator' that is adding up one benefit and comparing it with another only counts numbers; it has no sense of whether the benefit is small or large.

Going into town to a sale which offers £5 off is a good idea, perhaps, and it does not matter whether the £5 off is for an item which costs £6 normally, or an item which costs £600.

If the cheap calculator is given the figure of £5 off, it might value both equally, if it is given the figure as a % off, it might favour the £6 item.

In both cases it is a Right Hemisphere judgement of value triggered by Left Hemisphere 'counting'.

Your judgement is that personal purchasing is a complex situation except where something is driving the decision, e.g. a broken part for your lawn mower (which you have 'decided' to repair.

Facts, such as cost savings, might be entered into the scene, but your mental operations should moderate the value of that information.

So the advice is: Stay with the big picture and treat data, facts, information with great care, when the situation is truly complex.

Staying in a higher plane I probably achieved most easily with open processes like Synectics and CPS.

There may be good value in working at a lower plane for more 'data' based improvements, but this should be done only after the big picture solutions have been evaluated.

Collaboration and Competition

1. Collaboration

It is useful to separate our analysis between ***three types*** of collaboration.

The first is co-working with skills and knowledge, which no one individual has, to deliver a product or service within fairly well defined known boundaries.

A second is co-working for a broad 'fuzzily achieved' common mission where tasks, skills and knowledge are all overlapping.

Designing a next generation car would be of the first type, going for first place in a team competition in league football would be of the second kind.

A third type is where the co-working it itself designs the final outcome, people work together to create a product or service in which the value of the attributes are created alongside the outcome.

People fundraising and then getting built a community sports centre would be a project of the third kind.

In all situations competitive thinking may occur. A designer of one feature of the car may want to beat another in some kind of cost/benefit stand-off, more is spent on her design so less can be spent on his design.

A football player may sacrifice team performance for better chances of appearing to be the best player, by scoring goals perhaps.

This will be particularly true where performance is rewarded to individuals rather than teams, an all too common situation.

The same competitive element often enters community projects, unfortunately.

Where collaborative effort is required then that kind of competitive thinking and decision making will tend to be harmful.

Other features of collaborative thinking also need to be considered in all scenarios.

Collaborative effort works best if each mind has some awareness of the minds of others, so that the thinking and decision making of others is more easily understood.

In Synectics, the facilitator works to try to get people to be able to have a feel for the view of others but not to adopt an identical view. You see yourself having another view but you do not adopt that view.

If the thinking of one person is too greatly influenced by other perspectives then compromises will be built into that persons thinking and decision making.

You are accepting other views but managing the weighting given to them and their features. This is extended thinking about thinking.

If seeing other views leads to ready adoption then in the end everyone will be doing everyone else's job without doing their own to best advantage, a process which will often yield a mediocre solution.

So the designer of the bonnet catch will be designing for what they perceive to be the best bonnet design, and the footballer will be working too hard to get someone else to score a goal rather than score the goal themselves.

In a community sports centre every little option might be catered for, except the grand vision, which cannot be afforded, resources are spread around too thinly for best outcome.

If we return to our summary of judgement and decision making we can see how we might think about collaborative work:

"It is the collection of attributes which creates a collective aggregation of values which constitute judgements at various levels, in a multiple cross connection of minds, and the end decision has final value through some use of reason and intuition, but never reason alone."

Some degree of **_necessary distance_** is desirable at every stage of problem formulation, idea generation, idea selection and idea development right through to solution finding and selection.

'Necessary distance' is a concept developed by Iain McGilchrist, mentioned earlier. It is the old idea of either seeing the wood or the trees, but not both, which is what is needed.

Our management of our thinking in collaborative work especially needs some kind of reflection on the necessary distance we should keep from the thinking of other minds.

Close enough to have some feel but not so close that the valuations of thoughts and ideas of others takes over.

Some vision of the Community Sports Pavilion is needed, as well as someone thinking about pregnant mothers and access for wheelchairs.

The difference between collaboration where we combine use of skills and knowledge for a specific or broad team goal is the 'tolerance for failure' in the system.

You don't have to win every match to go top of the league, but you do have to have every part of a car fit together and work together.

So with collaborative effort with a specific goal there is going to be more reference to left hemisphere focussed thinking.

A common problem in that kind of teamwork is that the battle between one person's left hemisphere focus on one small element of the design against another person's grand holistic vision is not necessarily resolved.

Collaboration, a summary

Collaboration should be monitored and facilitated to allow management of 'necessary distance.' In the early stages the thinking work should be open, creative, allowing holistic thinking to lead.

In later stages the extent to which the left hemisphere focus is 'listened to' or valued, depends on how far the project is specific or general.

Footballers don't score goals by watching their feet, and cars don't exit the production line and work unless some pretty hard focus has been placed on every element and its implications.

One final point is that taking the line that people are multiply minded, a sound collaborative and healthy mind is one which allows each mind to listen to the others.

This can be facilitated by good mentoring, and can be self-mentored through use of note taking, diary keeping, sketch making, storyboarding.

Too often people are working in one conscious mode and feeling stressed because other minds are saying to them they want some air time, and some of these minds are in the same brain box! Take care of all your persona!

2. Competition

Competitive thinking is winner takes all. It may require putting together any number of pieces, but anyone, of many people, can put those pieces together, or many people can put it together.

The competitive thinking may be between ideas within one mind and one persona, betweenpersona in one brain of one person, and between persona of different people.

But the pieces which yield a solution might not fit without an enormous amount of mental effort. Paradigms have to be challenged, old value systems broken up. Courage is needed to propose the ridiculous, sometimes. And remember, this competition may be between persona across or within minds with different pieces coming together or conflicting all the time.

But the value of the attributes of the winning idea is not created by human minds, not directly anyway. If human minds are creating the winning idea then it is a collaborative outcome.

The winning idea, where ideas compete, ultimately exists out there in the laws of physics, chemistry, and biology, at basic level or as emergent properties in the evolution of systems.

These emergent properties may exist all the way up to the next fashion in clothes or cars or computer games, but they are real emergent properties, the mental operations in the mind are ones of discovery not creation. Ultimately creation is a collaborative activity, discovery is competition.

This kind of winner takes all thinking works very well with a substantial multilevel process such as TRIZ, which can dig deep and challenge to any level needed.

And this sounds like left hemisphere, focus, detail, reasoning, digging deeper and deeper.

If I was working within a competition to come up with the winning ideas I would definitely pick TRIZ as the process tool of choice.

And I would definitely be using focussed thinking a lot. So the only question is, is there any value in holistic thinking? Is the right hemisphere needed at all?

To answer this question we need to look at the possible faults of left brain focussed thinking.

Returning to the idea of focus as being able to work on numbers as an adding machine only, we can see that one danger is that the focus becomes one of satisfying the numbers rather than delivering real benefits.

The holistic thinking is needed to check that a solution is doing what it is really supposed to do in *adding value*.

Let's imagine an example which may not be so far from the truth. Suppose you want to create a database of all cars in a country, their tax status, their engine and registration details, and their owner's details.

Cataloguing all these is fairly simple and an algorithm is created which works well for 99.99999% of cases, meeting all the database size requirements, speed of operation and cost factors.

But the one car it cannot add to the system is a specially built Bugatti for Major General T J Thompson-McKinley-Smythe.

For one thing, the Bugatti has never had a model number, and in fact is not really a Bugatti as it was made ex works by staff from the company.

Also, the Major General has two elements to his name title and the database only really works with one, and it allows two 'Family Names' hyphenated, but not three.

The left hemisphere stays on target, works through algorithmic options and superbly computes additional special options with only a little extra cost, just 0.0001% of the overall cost, to complete the task.

But the right hemisphere, the one seeing the whole picture, may suggest another solution.

It says, 0.0001% of the cost is the salary of one person for a whole year, so how about we appoint one person on a part time basis to phone the Major General and get the car tax update each year personally?

The point of the story, I hope, is that ultimately the left hemisphere cannot be relied on to stay with a holistic view of value.

The numbers take over, the number of facts means more than the value of the facts. So some creative thinking, some holistic thinking is still needed.

Competition, a summary

Competition is ultimately a highly directed, focussed activity, a winner takes all, and mostly left brain. It may start with multiple focus points, but in the end draws down to just a few, then one.

But the right brain, the right hemisphere, with its holistic thinking is needed from time to time to make sure that the thinking has not left the real world altogether.

This is where some creative thinking work is done just to check all is OK.

And finally, if the competitive thinking seems to be delivering **All Gold** at very little cost, then one final check of Gut Feeling should be done.

Does this feel right? Can I trust it?

Maybe you can, and if the work has been done well it should be OK, but the final check before total commitment seems a good idea.

There is a lovely story of how a fairly nerdy professor had worked out all the parameters of a successful long term relationship.

The facts were there, he published them, and then he met someone and got married. He was asked if he used all his ideas in the choice.

Not at all, this was too important a decision to leave to theory!

Short term/medium term/long term and completion/progress

So how long before the solution is needed? How long is it supposed to last?

For short term goals we have a greater need for 'on task' thinking. People who are forever thinking up something new when there is 'a job to be done' get very annoying. Especially when a building is on fire!

Of course there may be a better way of doing things, but the risk is that any delay increases the risk of panic action at the end, with consequently higher cost.

Relaxed, holistic thinking takes time, does not always work to schedules, is more happenchance, and even though the benefits can be enormous, the risk is there that delay will occur if allowed too much reign.

The most appropriate thinking strategy where short term goals occur is to have done the relaxed, holistic creative thinking beforehand.

Then the only right hemisphere check is to see if the 'gut feeling' you have is sending any warnings that the pre-planned process for dealing with the short term goal is sending any warning signals, 'is there anything different which would not make this process work?

If no signals, then allow focussed work on getting things done.

For long term goals we have the luxury of allowing a lot of time for big thinking, suggesting that a number of open thinking tools like CPS, Synectics and even TRIZ used in an open facilitated session will pay back in time and effort and cost and benefit.

The left brain will be wanting to get stuck in there and analyse everything to death, so the choice to be made is how much time to give to details.

You may find that keeping the left brain quiet is hard work, and if so then allocated periods of focus are no bad thing, in fact the exploration of detail may be a catalyst for new thinking.

Usually, however, groups of minds tend to jump too readily into action mode, left brain takes over when much easier ways of resolving through to solution would have been found if open minds had stayed in charge.

And of course, for the medium term, your choice is somewhere in between.

The approach suggested is not to make out that everything is one side or the other, but that an awareness of how thinking works, and how group thinking works, and a clear decision to manage a switch between left and right brain thinking is no bad thing.

Sports Psychology and time frames - *Interpreting the terrain*

We are now looking to managing, as best we can, the machine that is our mind, the machine that is us.

Whether it is working out how to review our focussed, left brain kind of thinking or holistic, big picture, storyline right brain kind of thinking, or the two together, their interaction, a major part of this review is to understand the terrain, the context in which we are applying our thinking, and our thinking about our thinking.

The review of 'routine' situations in sport is well developed in the world of sport psychology and coaching.

Although suddenly finding oneself facing the world no 1 tennis champion, the review processes would be standard, with just a little out of the box thinking perhaps.

This is because, on court, as a player, you have to be drawing on complete and whole game skill sets. You cannot win a tennis match in left brain mode.

You might use left brain before the start of the match, in the build-up, but unless you are 110% on song with yourself when you start playing you will start losing.

The medium term and long term in sport does provide a different kind of terrain, one in which both hemispheres are to be used.

This is because the algorithm of play, and the algorithms of seasonal fixture programmes, introduce a complexity which warrants a wider review.

The possible tactics of all the players, and all the teams of players, yields a near infinite array of possibilities.

Determination

We all have an experience of our own determination to do things. But where does this determination reside?

It must in some ways represent brain energy, but how? Certainly we know that variation awakens brain energy and switching from LH to RH (and front to back, or between any different areas) is good practice, every 15 minutes probably.

But there is also something which occasionally holds focus on the medium to long term, whether in the final games of a tennis tournament or survival out on a raft, out at sea.

Such determination can be the avoidance of something, as when Hitler refused to see the defeat that was inevitable at the end of World War 2, which is a kind of determination NOT to face the truth, cognitive avoidance process.

And so, out at sea, or at the end of a tennis tournament, the determination not to be defeated can be the determination to avoid something unthinkable.

There is also a positive determination, which drives us to win, a mate, the best food, the highest status.

This is also RH material. The LH can't decide even between two colours. So somewhere in the right brain is our energy to continue, our energy to complete, all the way to the end.

Brain waves

A final note should be on how long it takes to switch from focus to open thinking.

It seems that these levels relate to the measurable regular frequencies of the brain, with sleep at 0 to 3 cps, dreaming at 3 to 7 cps, creative thinking at 7 to 14 cps and focused thinking at 14 to 28 cps.

We are built to switch easily from slow to fast, perhaps because if a danger occurs focussed thinking is needed, fight or flee, and if you are fighting that bear don't let creative thinking distract you too much (though the odd good idea may be worth it!)

We are not built to go easily from fast to slow, so while in idea sessions you can almost instantly get people into focussing on a particular issue, you need some exercise to get people back into slow, which could be just having fun, telling jokes, having a laugh, or could be going for a walk, having a shower, or just reading a book.

Risk type – catalytic or progressive, known/unknown ratio

Collaboration or competition, and short term to long term goals are both related to types of risk, but they don't cover all types of risk.

Collaboration vs. competition and short and long term goals are 'process speed' risks, a kind of people factor which does need to be considered as risk.

Also we have two other factors in risk:

1. Catalytic or progressive
2. Known and unknown

Catalytic and known

A catalytic risk occurs when a system has built in vulnerability. It might be a market vulnerability or an operational system vulnerability or it may be a product vulnerability, things will fail in certain circumstances.

Dealing with a known vulnerability is a standard problem solving exercise, and the types of cost benefit analysis using left and right brain are appropriate.

We know that the right brain will want to hold on to a current viewpoint and be blind to information which challenges that viewpoint. So the right brain is not listening to the left.

We also know that the left brain will be a bean counter and fail to see significance in change if the change seems to be small in terms of numbers.

If you need 100 litres of water to walk across a desert and lose 5 litres, you might end up dead, but the left brain will not be shouting that loud and clear, unless the framing has been adjusted in such a way as to indicate the number is important.

So the left brain needs to hear that the water for the last ten miles has ALL been lost, 100%, and it is the right brain which would suggest a way of capturing the importance of all the elements.

The whole picture needs to have value attributes which indicate true loss, as only that will trigger the kind of catalytic response the brain needs in such circumstances.

We also know that in group situations it will be the groups' value attributes which will prevail, and despite the possibility of there being wisdom in crowds there is also the possibility of stupidity in crowds.

Even if one mind has recognised the real value attributes of a situation, the end result will be a failure unless that person has ultimate power or unless they can change the value attributes of others, unless they can change how people FEEL about what is true.

It is not enough and never is enough to put forward anything that may appear to be facts.

People's decision making is not based on being right, only in being in agreement with the majority.

That is a fundamental problem with the brain, evolution has 'decided' that advantage lies in being with the majority, not being the one who is right.

If you are a lioness and you think it is clear that you should go for the smallest gazelle, but that will be of little use unless the others go with you.

The rules of the pack are pretty clear. This is why ostracism is so strong. We are pack thinking and decision makers.

Catalytic and unknown

One very interesting and challenging questions is, 'how do you know what you don't know?' This can be a question posed by someone who just wants to disagree with you, it is the question of universal uncertainty.

So in one sense it is unanswerable. But the interesting question is, 'what can you do to minimise risk from the unknown?'

Fans of TRIZ will know the main answer to this question, you build in gradual failure into the design.

If you make a 5 legged chair then on leg should fail if the system begins to be compromised.

If your market might have vulnerabilities in it then you have one part of the market slightly weaker so you get advance warning.

If the consequence of failure is severe then the effort put into covering all possibilities has to be much higher, but we have processes in TRIZ to cover those, and all we need is the additional cross checks between right and left brain thinking as noted earlier.

Finally, we have the big 'What if?' What if we still have missed something big?

As Gerd Gigerenzer points out in his book Gut Feelings, it is surprising how good your gut feel can be when things are complex and the unknown really does seem unknown.

Sometimes we will miss seeing the big thing because we have too many facts in front of us.

So when facing situations which could contain lots of unknowns, it is best to bring in facts slowly, if they come in too quickly they create formulations of the future which make a great picture or a great story, which has big holes in it.

Scree

Walking through the hills of Southern Spain, I became intrigued by the difficulty that loose terrain presents; in some places we would call it 'scree'.

The ground never settles. Large and small rocks and stones and loose powdery grain comes down from on high every time it rains heavily, so that nothing is reliable under foot.

It was easy to make comparisons with the current, 2011, turmoil in the markets.

Nothing seems firm under foot, a small step can lead to a collapse, a large weighty object can be a source of stability or a weight which brings down an avalanche (this thought occurs as I receive news that UBS seems to have lost 2 billion dollars in unauthorised trading, without noticing it.

To steady yourself on the mountain, it is wise to use two walking sticks, not one.

You need 4 points of stability reducing to 3 as you move. Hopefully only one foothold will give at a time and you test every single new point of contact as much as you can.

There is also the bigger picture. If the scree is ready to give then you make it give, up to a point. You dig in and it collapses, just a bit.

So in turmoil, it seems wise to judge how we use focus and how to set it in the bigger picture. Sometimes you are working at just one point at a time, measuring carefully each step.

At other times you test the system, you challenge the ground enough to stabilise it again.

Whether this means acquiring or selling significant assets or point by point testing of the market is a continuous judgement to make.

Occasionally the bigger picture says, if you can, get off this hill, it might collapse completely.

The state of mind needed to make continuous judgements in high risk, turmoil, where catastrophe is a possibility, is very different from the state of mind where freewheeling is the best option.

Turmoil and potential catastrophe requires care and deep judgement, not LH or RH but both, regularly, frequently, and interactively.

Summary

Understanding paradigms on thinking helps you frame how to think about your thinking.

Thinking may be focussed or holistic, and may occur in several of the minds of each person, and develop alongside and within the minds of others.

Thinking, leading to judgement of value attributes of things, is a dynamic concatenation of neural events for which people have little specific control.

Managing one's thinking is about matching thinking processes to task types, to risk types, to speed of need and to the extent of collaborative activity.

Understanding this means that a framework can be established on how you will check your focussed thinking, and how you will check your holistic thinking, what tools you will use.

On how frequently you will use one side of the brain to check the other, and how frequently you will use it to check what is going on on the same side.

So focussed thinking can check focussed thinking, and holistic thinking can check focussed thinking, and vice versa.

We have been making big mistakes as individuals and as a society, with leaders and people who follow, and the big mistakes in part have just been having the wrong paradigms about thinking.

In the 21st Century, it is time to adopt a real science of thinking, judgement and decision making.

How to practise your 21st Century Thinking

1. Consciousness is a multi - mind, multilevel operation, don't think focus is always a good thing, think broadly and deeply or in focus by choice of mind and choice of level of awareness.
People are capable of using many different persona, personality tests have wrongly suggested people are a single profile of traits and proclivities.

2. Be aware that your thoughts take on judgement attributes differently in different minds; different minds recall different memories and skills.
Choose minds variously for different parts of a task as well as for different tasks.

3. Be aware that your thoughts and their judgement attributes coexist across the minds of others, that this is useful in part.
Choose how much you allow a nudge of judgements when listening to and recording the judgement attributes of others.

Think about how your judgement attributes are influencing others, in collaboration or competition.

4. Listen to the parts and the whole, observe the parts and the whole, have a feel for the parts and the whole.
Thinking at its best is being inside and outside your mind and its relationship with what is there.

5. Use multiple toolkits for thinking alongside recording processes, from diaries with words and sketches, to mind-mapping software and hardware, to process toolkits like Synectics, TRIZ, CPS and Lateral Thinking.
Match the tools to the thinking processes and be aware of how each influences the other.

6. Watch out for the common errors of left brained focussed thinking.
LH thinking by numbers and segregated parts and valuing everything equally.
Errors of right brained thinking - over-simple imagery and sticking to that in defiance of numbers, facts, observations - cognitive dissonance.

7. Work out and continue to modify how you perceive the context of the problem, issues,

opportunities, the complexity, the collaboration/competition, the time scales and the risk factors.
Choose minds and thinking tools which match those aspects of context and change as needed as the task progresses.

8. If you are the boss, remember that it would be better for those who work for you to be thinking about their thinking than you telling them how to think.
Your job is to think about how to think about their thinking. That's why you get paid what you do.

Tips

1. When you start the day, have a think about what kind of mind, what kind of consciousness you might be needing.
The most important decision of the day may be how you start it!

2. At your desk, on your wall, in your pocket, have some kind of symbol, maybe some beads to count, something which occasionally wakes you up and asks you to consider: Is it turning out the kind of day you were expecting?
Is some kind of change of mind needed? Am I awake? Should I be awake?

3. When you map your tasks for the day, put some 'context symbols' next to them to help you decide what kind of mind you will best use for each of them.
Risk, known unknown, long/short term, compete or collaborate and complexity.

4. If anything looks really bad, ask yourself if it is time to see if a creative solution can bring things back in control.
Creative solutions tend to bring energy from other parts of the brain.

5. At the end of the day review how it went with your state of mind, with your actions and outcomes, with how you managed process, with how accurate your view of Context was.

6. From time to time, ask yourself: 'am I listening to others?' and 'am I listening to my various 'selves'?'

From where I am sitting

Those who have started learning Spanish will have, perhaps, struggled to remember 'sentar', to sit, or be seated, and 'sentir' to feel. There are also the verbs asentar and asentir with similar meanings.

Part of the difficulty may be that actually to be seated and to have a "viewpoint" is closer in meaning to feel than seems initially apparent.

My guess is that for the Spanish, the difference is even less, which is why the words are similar, and sentar bien means to sit well, and to have a good opinion of something.

The LH, wanting focus, separation, abstraction, and universals, has a problem with viewpoints, which seem subjective.

In some ways, but not all ways, the process of science is to objectify, to remove the subjective, though as science advances, such as in medicine, evolution and relativistic physics;the subjective seems to push its nose in again and again.

The RH, taking a holistic view, finds context to be naturally part of the sense of understanding of things.

It is perhaps interesting that the language used in the process called Synectics takes on a personal perspective.

Participants in groups are encouraged strongly, to use the word 'I', and not 'we' or 'it'. So someone who says "So how I see it is …" or "How it looks to me is …" and even "From where I am sitting …".

Use of role play allows displacement of personal perspective, from the straightforward "If I were the customer I would …." To the more playful, "If I were a brick on the corner of the building I would …".

Playful use of language allows the LH analysis to remain conceptually embedded within the bigger picture.

Everyone knows it is a single perspective, so LH dominance in the long term can hopefully be avoided.

Finally:

1. **People don't care about being wrong**

The brain is designed to value consensus more than correctness; if you are not with the group your survival is threatened.

You will find it hard to tackle this head on. Because it is not how the brain works, you are trying to change a machine that will only nudge itself into change.

2. **The Bigger the Reaction to some idea the more you should wake up to why!**

If your feeling is shouting NO, then it is because some part of you is shouting MAYBE YES?

If you see someone who is showing their feelings are shouting NO then explore how it may be that some part of them, one persona or just the other hemisphere is shouting MAYBE YES.

This is something to explore not confront.

Finally, a quote:

"Before you diagnose yourself with depression or low self-esteem, first make sure that you are not, in fact, just surrounded by assholes." - William Gibson

How to Advise The President

Climate Change: High risk/unknowns, Catastrophic, Catalytic, Collaborative, Complex

Need:

1. Creative exploration of risks and options, a lot to begin with and then repeated at intervals.
2. Extensive cross checking between reason and intuition, each against the other, awareness of possible false valuation of numbers, awareness of false 'big pictures'/cognitive dissonance, exploration of what are the unknowns.
3. Regular and Frequent Reality Checks, is mental drift occurring?
4. Frequent cross checks on thinking about other people's thinking, what do they think you are thinking and how clear are you about what they are thinking.
5. Check if people care about being wrong and ask why! Losing group consensus or drifting from what is true?
6. Stand back when big emotional reactions occur. Find out why.
   Especially, do you know intuitively some unknowns that you are not putting down on paper? Perceptual avoidance is possible and maybe likely.

7. Keep asking: 'Are things getting done?' 'Are they the right things?' Listen to reason and listen to intuition. Rely on neither.
8. Avoiding risk may be greater than taking a risk. Is the judgement of risk being played down? If risk is catalytic and catastrophic do you need to adopt a total single-mindedness to risk reduction than multi-minded, collaborative efforts to reduce current harm?

Given complexity of enormous proportions, it seems foolish to think that you will ever find an expert who 'knows the answer.'

In highly complex situations (one's which are truly complex and not just have unknowns), experts are best used briefly to assist in generating a range of hypotheses and this leads to a range of actions, none of which should be too expensive as all need to be tried.

Money is saved on not paying much to experts because they are used briefly and intensively rather than extensively.

If, however, the risk assessment suggests near term, catalytic, catastrophic outcomes then a mental switch may be needed to focus (and gamble) entirely on one strategy and make it happen, single-mindedly.

So the advice to The President is, spend a little money on getting advice from lots of people, treat them all as speculative, and spend money trying out all those that seem to have any chance of success.

The cost benefit ratio comes from spread betting, but huge returns on the winner.

Once a winning formula seems to be emerging, then the action set, the thinking set may change, you no longer may have the complex, collaborative change programme but the risk of failure may remain high.

Employment: Low risk/slow change, Collaborative, Complex

Need:

1. Emphasis on creative and intuitive, take time to get it right.
2. Keep asking with personal interest: 'Are things getting done?' 'Who is deciding if they are the right things?'
3. As change is slow, working on Eco Mind Sets is where long term progress will be made.
4. Unknowns become knowns 'after the fact.' Learning is by exploration into new territory.

Because employment overall changes slowly and in a complex way, there will be many people from many organisations, public and private, who want to sell the idea of quick fixes.

The brain is so heavily designed around simplification that people want to offer it and people want to receive it, against all evidence to the contrary. The brain is oriented towards consensus rather than reality.

As change in any employment programme will be slow there will be a relentless push for simplicity. Determination is needed to stay away from the idea of quick fixes.

The brain will be tempted to take quick fixes from left and right hemispheres.

From reasoning there will be a temptation to over value small changes in numbers, from intuition the desire to see positive change will mean it will be seen whether it is there or not.

A good check is to ask, if tempted into seeing positive change, which Mind you are in which sees this positive change.

You can role play another mind, a sceptical mind, and ask 'their' view. Then try to weigh up which view seems to be best balanced in weighing up the evidence, for reason and for intuition!

Riots: High Risk, mixed known and unknown, Catalytic Change, Collaborative, Complex
Need:

1. Creative exploration of risks and options. The many forms rioting can take needs a lot of scenario work to begin with.
2. Some cross checking between reason and intuition, each against the other. Awareness of possible false valuation of numbers, (small crowds have created revolutions, big crowds have withered and died), awareness of false 'big pictures'/cognitive dissonance, seeing the crowd as all of the same kind.
3. Regular Reality Checks, is mental drift occurring?
4. Frequent cross checks on thinking about other people's thinking, what do they think you are thinking and how clear are you about what they are thinking – this is where things are most likely to be fatally wrong.
5. Stand back when big emotional reactions occur, yours and others'. Find out why. The answers could be many and confusing.
6. Keep asking: 'Are things getting done?' 'Are they the right things?' Listen to reason and listen to intuition. Rely on neither.
7. Try to minimise the unknown, gather data but keep its meaningfulness in perspective.

It is interesting that professional reports, including those from the profession of psychology, have mixed paradigms on riots.

For evolutionary psychology we have suggestions that crowds have some kind of feral link to people historically, animalistically working in packs.But these packs seem to be working on some kind of cost-benefit equation.

So we have a report in the November 2011 edition of The Psychologist, that 66% of rioters in London were under 25, 90% were male, and 41% were from 'the most deprived areas' of the UK.

The argument suggested is a rational one, "violence is not always pathological but facultive and strategic." "A Facultive strategy will only stabilise if it has a net positive effect on average lifetime inclusive fitness."

So now you know! "Little to lose and everything to gain."

Clearly the paradigm is close to the Eco Minded reasoning outline earlier in this book. The Eco mind is behaving 'rationally'.

The danger of a thinking error is to treat input and outcome as if it was dealing with an individual. Can the Eco Mind you are dealing with really be reduced to simple equations?

It may appear so complex that nothing can be done, but Governments around the world tackled smoking in public very successfully, after decades of trying to change individual's behaviour the behaviour of groups was tackled head on and with little problem. (See Health, Smoking and Behaviour Change).

Health: Low risk, collaborative, complex/simple mix, known/unknown mix, progressive change

Need:

1. A mixture of analytic focussed thinking and holistic open thinking.
2. A Multiplicity viewpoint, recognition that people have healthy minds and unhealthy minds, or at least minds which put health and safety lower down the rankings of importance.
3. A regular and frequent adjustment of what constitutes a necessary distance from the issues, problems, opportunities.
4. Where possible try to convert unknown into known but beware of false positives judged high value by desire to have simple outcomes.

Because the change is progressive and because some health issues may be relatively simple (if you can find the scientific answer all of one kind of problem may be solved).

Others will be immensely complex (such as obesity, seemingly) the first progression plan for thinking about thinking, valuing, making judgements, leading to decisions, is the separation where possible of the simple and the complex.

Basically, if simple may be possible try it.

An intuitive check is needed to ensure that the judgement that it is simple is not because you and others want it to be simple, but if that checks out OK then that stream should be separated out and funded differently.

Some of the complex issues may be simpler than it seemed. So somehow masses of left brained messages to people about the dangers of smoking pretty much failed.

The arguments that smoking cut your life span, lead to horrid, painful illnesses, reduced sexual potency and many other similar messages had little effect (though some effect it is agreed.)

But a simple ban of smoking in public places lead to very little protest.

This was despite many left brained 'rational' arguments against it:

1. Loss of business
2. It is contrary to basic principles of free choice of behaviour
3. The evidence for 'passive smoking' is much less significant than for active smoking
4. If people had not believed the latter why should they believe the former?

So we had a complex, collaborative project which was essentially 'solved' to some degree by a simple set of actions.

It would have been hard, maybe impossible, to truly predict the outcome. That is the nature of complex, collaborative problems, but it was 'worth the experiment', because for the cost the outcome exceeded expectations.

Where the situation is progressive it is possible to try many different strategies without ever knowing which one might work.

Having eliminated the simple, it is perhaps best that Gerd Gigerenzer's advice to trust Gut Feel is best.

Though this does need checking as things change and the check need to be on the intuition, does it still feel right?

And with left brained focused examination of evidence. Do the numbers add up? (And if not, maybe they weren't the right numbers, so check against check against check for complex and collaborative projects.)

Despite this being a complex issue requiring collaborative approaches the emphasis on numbers has been extraordinary.

From the simple 5 a day campaigns for eating fruit and veg to the 1 or 2 units of alcohol maximum to the calorie counting, carb counting protein counting diets, the increase in obesity may be as much to do with the emphasis on numbers and away from the holistic viewpoint as anything else.

It is perhaps the use of the wrong kind of minds that has led to the current health issues. People see health as being what other people, experts, deliver through provision of drugs, eating and exercise controlled regimes and more.

It is good evidence that having the wrong mind on the job leads to failure.

Education: Low risk, slow change, complex, mostly knowns, collaborative

Need:

1. Intuitive, collaborative thinking, leadership through development of Eco Mind thinking.
2. Be wary of evaluation by reasoning, good practice is mostly known, adoption and implementation has been the problem.
3. A good sense of 'necessary distance', close enough to be engaged but far enough away to see how Education, and Learning, are deeply embedded in everything.

The expression that 'it takes a whole village to bring up a child' indicates how holistic education is, how collaborative, how much it is about Eco Minds not Egos.

Yet competitive thinking is woven through most education systems. Winners and losers, scales of performance, are endemic in every part of the education system and are embedded in the minds of children, young people and parents.

Yet the history of most great thinkers suggests more a rejection of that kind of thinking, often with people like Einstein being failures in the system as often as succeeders.

The fact that education is low risk but slow change, complex and collaborative makes it clear that competitive thinking is likely to be disruptive and harmful.

Societies' failure to take a 'necessary distance' with respect to education and learning in general is an indication of **how great the failure of the thinking, judgement and decision making can be,** by leaders, managers and the general public.

Crime: Complex, collaborative, progressive, low risk (mostly)

Need:

1. Multiplicity thinking, good guys are also bad guys and vice versa, often, not all minds play out.

2. Abandonment of reason, crime is not a reasoned act, mostly, and almost never simple.
3. To 'Walk in the shoes of the criminal', metaphorically.
4. Use toolkits to map the multilevel and multi-mind nature of crime.
5. Use creativity to bring new energy to ideas and actions.
6. Frequent cross checks on thinking about other people's thinking, what do they think you are thinking and how clear are you about what they are thinking – this is where things are most likely to be fatally wrong.
7. Explore where the necessary distance is to get the best view or to find many different views (which may vary from one type of crime to another).

Having a religious right or wrong element to crime makes the complexity more complex for necessary distance.

It is not easy to find a good distance for 'empathy', meaning having some kind of intuitive feel for the criminal act and criminal mind. We have been trained not to look at it as anything other than bad.

This feeling of being forced to judge is hard to dismantle, but as seen in processes of reparation for ethnic violence on a grand scale or simple face to face meetings with victims, they can be the most rewarding.

So to 'judge' the crime and the criminal, as a generic act or in particular, we cannot use reason, in the end numbers have minimal meaning.

So it is necessary to find the mind inside ourselves which can take that view from the necessary distance, which can find an empathy, which of course does not mean forgiveness.

Creative reframing of crime is not implying excuses or escape; it is applying multiplicity of minds to positive outcomes, staying clear of judgement by numbers and by reason alone.

Mostly crime at lower levels has many knowns, a big database of knowledge exists. I do not know how much is known of organised crime at an International level.

War: Simple, competitive, short term, high risk, unknown

Need:

1. Focus, reason, information from the past, present and future.
2. Thinking toolkits for creative and analytical thinking, mind mapping of ideas.

3. Careful check on intuitions, feelings, using different Minds to review those.
4. Reason used to check reason, checklists for checklists.
5. Determination matched by open and detailed evaluation of progress, listening to the data and listening to what you hear about the data.
6. Frequent trials of moving the necessary distance back and forth to see how the picture changes, how the RH tells a different picture.

It may seem strange to declare war as simple and short term is of course a matter of degree. Keeping the peace is complex but in my judgement, war is simple.

Of course this is my judgement, this is what I would decide before choosing on that basis what kind of mental operations to apply, but perhaps more needs to be said.

Gianni Riotta, in his novel Prince of the Clouds, tells of someone who has studied war over centuries. The portrait is of games of chess, not easy games because of the risk and the 'unknowns'.

But the unknowns are unknown because it is hard to compute all the options, not because eventually the algorithms are unavailable.

Start with the idea of attrition, add a little game theory and there may even be an element of luck appearing, but needing to be lucky does not make something complex.

The spin of a coin never gets complex, so complexity and unknowns and luck are not linked directly.

The thinking strategies best applied for the simple, competitive, short term with some unkowns is creativity developed with sound procedural quality assurance processes, so, for example, a mixture of Synectics (always at the beginning) and TRIZ, with some Synectics threaded through as well.

Holistic thinking is useful to help manage the strategy but not to determine it.

All decisions will be judgement resulting from some kind of valuing of aspects of the plan, but it will be the focus and attention to detail, many details creatively explored as different scenarios, but details nonetheless which lead to success and failure in war.

Other areas

It is possible to look at all others areas of governance, of a company or a country. So we could look at Transport, Food Supply, Monetary Systems, Housing, and even things like Well Being.

The value in exploring the context of each of them lies in being able then to reflect on the thinking process that are appropriate and the checks against error that might especially be needed.

There is no absolute right or wrong on this, but it seems wise to have a process for thinking about thinking simply so that we can learn how that thinking works or does not work.

The main aim is to learn and improve.

Advice to Advisors to The President

The job of President is clearly complex, whether it is of a company or country (and of course this applies to Prime Ministers and other roles of major leadership).

Such leaders are challenged in ways to suggest that they have to justify actions by reason.

Yet because of the complexity, the judgement calls are really to the essence of judgement that those leaders apply.

Judgements on how well they are standing at a necessary distance from situations to be able to see them as best they can, so that the judgement call is as comprehensive as possible.

Presidents have to be Multi Minded, Eco Minded, but also have to be Ego Minded, or leadership would wander from day to day and week to week.

Presidents have to be close to people yet far enough away to see the crowd. Presidents have to be open to the creative idea yet wary of anything which is too attractively simple.

Presidents have to be able to use reason to avoid the ridiculous yet stand back from reason when reason alone seems to be leading down a path which intuition suggests is wrong.

Advisors to The President have in some ways an even more difficult job, unless they are only there for short term gain, as risk takers hoping for high stake returns.

The truly ethical advisor needs to have all the skills of The President and to be able to take a necessary distance from those skills to judge the skills themselves.

They have to understand how the application of those skills is a bias to judgement itself, things delivered well will be weighted more than things which were not so well presented.

Robert Kegan, in his book, In Over our Heads, speaks about how we need level 5 thinking skills to even handle the interchange with our teenage children.

We need to be able to think about how they think about what we think they are thinking. And we need to be able to think about that thinking before we can make choices.

How much more difficult it is to be Advisor to the President.

The various tools and techniques that have been developed in this book will hopefully assist, but they need practice. Practice starts best at an early age.

The first job for an Advisor to The President is perhaps to help the President see the value of thinking about thinking.

Thinking about thinking at the beginning of all education, at every stage in education, to learn about learning we begin with lessons in thinking about thinking, judgement, and decision making.

Afterword 1 – Poverty

Poverty is often in the news in the UK and around the world, and always there is some confusion about what it really means, what is really important.

It might be useful to explore what poverty means in terms of how our minds work, how when 'resource poor' or when 'resource rich' we engage different kinds of thinking.

Poverty meaning lack of money, assets, is clearly a risk factor, there are things you cannot do. So having some 'reserves' seems sensible.

But poverty of spirit, the lack of emotional reserves seems often to be just as damning if not more so. And they are linked.

If poverty in economic terms is linked to frequent and unpredictable hits on income or production for self-sufficiency, then people will feel high levels of stress, because of high levels of threat.

Focusing on threat moves in to a point where any joy, any energy is lost. This is because focus is a left brained operation and tends to be energy draining.

If nothing spins back to the right brain then the energy to continue drains away.

When people say they are 'ground down' this is an accurate picture as it reflects a bit by bit wearing down, lots of tiny pieces being taken off till we are 'down to the bone.'

Creative and holistic experience of being at one with the world is lost, as the right brain/right hemisphere does not get access.

Interestingly, if income is higher but debt and risk are also higher then the results may be the same, so we have a wealth in economic terms but a poverty of experience.

Where people are economically poor but have good control of their core needs, especially where risk is reduced by family or community, then people can feel life is rich in experience.

Being rich in experience and money is possible of course, but only if threat is managed and risks low, to allow enough right brain experience.

Afterword 2 – Ecce Homo

These thoughts below were inspired by a most beautiful book, Prince of the Clouds, by Gianni Riotta.

In that book a Colonel Terzo tries to reconstruct a way of living based on analysing and understanding warfare over thousands of years, always wondering if method or madness is the script which succeeds.

Science is most certainly based on method, but also, perhaps, for the occasional breakthrough, on madness as well.

Mostly science takes small steps with the collection of data providing a pathway to progress slowly and surely.

Occasionally the data collection builds up like the pressure of water on a dam, and the dam collapses.

Occasionally science surrenders after the challenge of trying to understand exceptional cases, things that happen which seem to confound theory.

These are the cracks in the dam, which were present when the dam was built but not seen.

In the process of science more data is collected in relation to this challenge of the exceptional case, such as the theory of tectonic plates which explains the shifting of the continents and also odd patterns in different lands in the evolution of animals.

Or we have the Michelin-Morley experiment which failed to find the 'true movement' of the earth through the ether, leading to the theory of relativity, and lately we have the absence, as seems to be the case at the point of writing this, of the Higgs Boson.

As a psychologist of the mind, there are many exceptional abilities which challenge orthodox thinking in psychology.

The simple case of how a tennis player manages to return a ball travelling at 120 mph, or a goalkeeper parries a shot from an attacker just yards away, these are hard to understand and explain either as feats of prediction or as neural responses and muscle action.

Even harder to understand is the development of language in barely formed brains, or the intuitive sense of mathematics or the seemingly inspired ability to read minds, to some degree a skill present from birth.

Having a special interest in autism I have always been puzzled by the amazing skills that are occasionally shown in art and mathematics by such children.

Some autistic children draw not only a technically correct perspective but draw in a way which suggests mature understanding of affect, such as Nadia's horse which is alive and has feelings.

A final puzzle of a different kind has for me been religious and spiritual interpretations of the world.

Some could be explained as simply the evolution of complex societies, an invention of solutions to mysteries of the world, life and death, and of course consciousness.

But sometimes things occur which are much harder to explain, a thought triggered by the words, Ecce Homo, in the book, Prince of the Clouds.

To be human, not just to be conscious, where do myth and reality co-align? For me, one element of this religious mystery is the co-existence framework for God as The Father, The Son and The Holy Spirit.

How do I make sense of that? But a concept of triage is well formed in many societies.

Whether it is King, Parliament and the Church, or 2 Parliaments and a Justice System, as in the UK and USA.

It is easy to understand how 2 parties can conspire naturally for their mutual benefit, but not to understand The Father, The Son and The Holy Spirit.

So I wonder if it is fair and reasonable to compare notes with the brain sciences. We have, throughout this book, compared the focused analytical thinking of the LH with the holistic RH. So where is the triage?

If we think of The Father as the holistic thinker, the Son as the pragmatic activist based on detail (even down to the number of talents a person has!) then we have left some essence of what it is as the Human Spirit.

So it is the Human Spirit which, in exercising Judgement, between the two hemispheres, between the holistic thinker and the pragmatist, that balances things, and makes us truly, what it is as Ecce Homo, to be human.

www.ingramcontent.com/pod-product-compliance
Lightning Source LLC
Chambersburg PA
CBHW071034240526
45469CB00006BD/2203